HELPING CHILDREN LEARN TO READ THROUGH MULTI-SENSORY READING ACTIVITIES

A HANDBOOK AND RESOURCE GUIDE FOR PARENTS AND TEACHERS

Carol Fraser Hagen M.A. Ed.S.

GW00568416

Learning Press

HELPING CHILDREN LEARN TO READ THROUGH MULTI-SENSORY READING ACTIVITIES

A HANDBOOK AND RESOURCE GUIDE FOR PARENTS AND TEACHERS

Carol Fraser Hagen M.A. Ed.S.

Published by Learning Leaf Press in conjunction with Summer Bay Press.

Editing, Interior Design and Cover Design:
Wendy Dewar Hughes, Summer Bay Press

ISBN: 978-0-9897742-0-8
Digital ISBN: 978-0-9897742-1-5

www.carolfraserhagen.com

With love to my son, John, - CFH

CONTENTS

ii

FOREWORD

Helping Children Learn to Read through Multisensory Reading Activities, by Carol Fraser Hagen is a great resource for parents and professionals. Whether this is your first time or have had experience guiding young readers, you will enjoy the activities offered in this book.

Carol has used her years of experience as a reading educator to create a book that is filled with activities that promote reading.

She combines classic books for pre-readers through advanced levels with hands on learning activities. The ideas are practical and can be carried out with little expense.

Carol combines her technology expertise and knowledge of teaching to help promote reading for all ages.

Parents are a child's first teacher and reading begins well before children begin their school years. Parents can find suggestions on selecting a book and activities that will enrich their child's development.

Reading is the foundation of all learning and Carol's book helps open the door to the wealth of literature available to those that want to build that foundation.

Are you ready to have some fun? Read on!

Pam Dudley, Learning Language Expert, Dyslexia Tutor,
and Executive Director of Learning Abilities.
www.learningabilities.net

A NOTE TO PARENTS AND TEACHERS

In the 21st century, reading is a big part of everyday life throughout most of the world. As computers, cell phones, and other technology become more commonplace, most everyone needs to know how to read to make the most of this ever-changing technology. Text messages, email, and even social networking sites such as Facebook and Twitter all require the ability to read – on some level. This is actually good news. It means literacy is becoming a more authentic part of our world, not just something needed on the job or at school. We learn to read in order to have richer, more interesting lives, and books, magazines, and newspapers are just some of the many things we read every day.

With all this in mind, it's no wonder many parents want to know how they can supplement the reading instruction their child is receiving at school. And classroom teachers, who aren't designated "reading" teachers, also want to know how they can reinforce the concepts and skills children are learning through their schools' reading programs. This book was written with those parents and teachers in mind. This book was not written to teach children to read or correct reading problems, but supplement current classroom reading lessons.

The activities provided within this book are designed to help children improve their reading development and encourage a positive attitude toward learning and loving to read.

Parents who participate in their child's education – whether or not they homeschool their children – tend to produce children with better grades, better attitudes toward school and education in general.

You don't need any teaching experience to make the most of this book. You just have to have a desire to help your child and spend time together in a fun, but purposeful way.

"Parents play roles of inestimable importance in laying the foundation for learning to read. A parent is a child's first tutor in unraveling the fascinating puzzle of written language. A parent is a child's one enduring source of faith that somehow, sooner or later, he or she will become a good reader." (Becoming A Nations of Readers, 1985)

WHY I WROTE THIS BOOK

I have written this book for several reasons. First, as a Reading Specialist for more than ten years my classroom experiences teaching reading taught me how to identify critical milestones and good teaching practices, which are absolutely necessary for children to become better readers.

Second, throughout my teaching career parents, grandparents, friends and strangers, who learn I am a reading specialist, approach me for advice on what they can do to help their child, grandchild, niece, nephew, etc. become better readers.

Third, because I know the key to academic success is the ability to read well in order to understand the massive amounts of material children must read, throughout their school years.

Finally, I am passionate about books and reading. Naturally, I want every child to become an accomplished reader who discovers the pleasure of reading wonderful stories and about interesting subjects.

HOW TO USE THIS BOOK

This book contains activities, lists of recommended books, and other resources that parents or teachers can use to enhance whatever curriculum is being used to teach their children or students to learn how to read. All the activities and resources in this book are grouped for different ages and reading ability levels of children from babyhood through elementary school.

For example, activities and other resources for babies through toddlers are found in Part One of this book, while activities and resources for elementary school aged students who are struggling readers are found in Part Five.

It is suggested that parents and teachers read through each section of this book to learn the important milestones children are expected to reach at each level of their reading development and the problems children can experience at each level. Then the parent or teacher can turn to the section of this book that provides activities and other resources for the age and reading level of the child or student they are working with. Many of the activities in this book can be used with children at different stages in their reading development, which is why you'll see some of the same activities listed in different sections of this book.

The main thing I hope you will realize after reviewing this handbook and resource guide is that your attitude (as a parent and/or teacher) plays a big role in the way your child or student(s) develop(s) as a reader. If you have a positive attitude about reading and writing and learning in general, then your child will tend to grow up with the same positive attitude. Also, your attitude is reflected in the things you do as well as the things you say. If you say you enjoy reading, yet your child never sees you reading anything for pleasure, then it won't take long for your child to realize that your positive attitude about reading is little more than empty words. For that reason, be sure you also "model" your positive attitude about reading FOR your child. Be sure your child sees you reading and writing and enjoying these activities as often as possible.

MULTI-SENSORY TEACHING TECHNIQUES AND READING ACTIVITIES

Multi-sensory teaching techniques address all the learning pathways within the brain: seeing, hearing, touching and muscle memory. Because children have their own unique learning styles and needs, reading lessons are most effective using multi-sensory reading activities.

LEARNING STYLES

Children learn differently. Some children are visual learners (they need to "see" things that relate to what they are learning). Others are auditory learners (they need to "hear" things that relate to what they're trying to learn). This book addresses every style of learning with multi-sensory activities. Throughout this book you will see a small graphic next to each activities provided within each section. In fact the beauty of all the activities presented, are many reach more than one style of learner.

GRAPHICS THROUGHOUT THIS BOOK

The **Eye** 👁 indicates this is an activity that appeals to visual learners.

The **Ear** 👂 indicates this is an activity that appeals to auditory learners.

The **Hand** ✍ indicates this is an activity that appeals to learners who learn best with hands on activities, such as: writing, cutting and pasting.

The **Arm** 💪 indicates this is an activity that appeals to learners who learn best with activities require them to use physical activity, such as, moving around the room.

UNDERSTANDING READING GRADE LEVELS

Your school district provides your child with a reading literature book. This book, and unfortunately many elementary teacher misunderstand this, is written for student's **instructional level**. It's natural if students cannot read their literature books without mistakes. Grade level literature books are written slightly above grade level to stretch the reading growth of students.

On the other hand if a student can barely read their grade level literature book then it is considered to be on their **frustration level.** These students may need to work with the school's Reading Specialist. This teacher will help them re-learn prerequisite skills within learning to read, while bringing their reading achievement up to their expected grade level.

Conversely, if a student reads their reading literature book with ease, rapidly without mistakes, then we can assume they are reading above their grade level — on their **independent level.** In this instance children need to be given another book that challenges their reading development, or often they become bored and under achieve.

To find out what level your child is, sit down with him or her and his or her reading literature book. With these brief guidelines determine for yourself at what level you think your child reads. If you're still unsure or concerned talk to your child's teacher, and ask for a reading assessment. Finally, make sure you have your child's vision and hearing checked. These two tests are often overlooked and the results can turn your child's frustrations in learning to read, to success.

Finally, struggling readers often have poor "phonemic awareness". This simply means your struggling reader still has trouble hearing the succinct sounds the letters of the alphabet make. Additional practice, usually with the school's Reading Specialist, helps remediate this problem.

PART ONE

FOR PRE-READERS
READING MILESTONES FOR BABIES AND TODDLERS

You might not realize it but even babies and toddlers reach important reading milestones. These milestones actually prepare them to become readers.

Babies as young as a few months to one year usually begin to imitate sounds they hear in language. They respond when someone speaks to them. They also enjoy stories that are read to them, and may reach for books when someone is reading and even turn the pages with a little help.

As babies become toddlers, they are usually able to identify objects in books when someone reading to them opens a picture book about a dog, for example, and asks "Where's the dog?" or "What does a dog say?"

Toddlers also start to point at objects to identify them, and they may even pretend to read books if they have been read to on a regular basis. They realize reading is an important and enjoyable activity. They may also have a favorite book at this point and ask a parent, grandparent, teacher, or other caregiver to read it to them quite often.

The activities, suggested books, and other resources listed on the following pages were all compiled or created in order to help children at this stage – the pre-reading stage – get ready to learn to read.

ACTIVITIES FOR PRE-READERS

12 Fun Games, Puzzles, and Other Activities for Babies and Toddlers

Here are just a few of the many fun and instructional games, puzzles, and other activities you can enjoy with babies and toddlers. Once you try some of these games and activities, you may develop your own variations that personalize them just a bit more to make them more enjoyable for you and your children or students.

1. **Tent Reading** – This is a fun activity for school, a daycare center or at home.

First: Select a colorful and lively illustrated picture book such as, *Where's My Teddy*, by Jez Alborough.

Next: Make a tent out of blankets or sheets draped over a card table, your dining room or kitchen table. With your child or pre-school students, crawl into the tent and get comfy.

Begin: Read aloud, using good expression in your voice, point out and talk about the illustrations.

During Reading: Talk about the characters and what's going on in the story. Ask your child, or pre-school students, to make predictions. Such as, "What do you think is going to happen next?" Making predictions helps children develop good story comprehension. This is an enjoyable way to read aloud. Children see that reading is fun! That's important. This activity also helps them discover they can learn from books.

By the way, don't be surprised if your child, or pre-school student, wants you to read this book again. In fact, they may want you to read it over and over. Often children memorize stories and know exactly when to turn to the next page, and can even read it aloud themselves. However, they're really not reading. These smart pre-readers have the book memorized. Boy! Does this ever make them proud!

Special Note: Many children learn through their sense of touch. Parents and teachers should always try to meet the learning needs of every child with each learning activity. For example, with this activity consider providing a soft, fuzzy bear for that child who learns better through the sense of touch, while you're reading this wonderful story about a bear's teddy bear.

2. **Mock Reading** – Read a short, easy picture book (one that your child loves) over and over to your child. Use your finger to point at the words in the story as you read to the child. After your child has heard the story dozens of time, ask her if she would like to read the story to you. Give your child the book and let her turn the pages and "say" the story to you, as if she were actually reading. Next, let your child "read" the story into a tape recorder. Play the recording back so you child can hear herself "read." She'll be so proud of herself and this will reinforce the belief that reading and learning can (and should be) fun.

3. **Magnetic Spelling** – Purchase an inexpensive set of magnetic letters and numbers to place on your refrigerator. Use them to spell out your child's name. Next, spell out your child's pet's name. Use the letters to leave messages for your child such as: "Hello, Mark! "or "Good morning!" Encourage your child to ask you how to spell easy words. Then say these words and spell them with the letters and leave them in place on your refrigerator for a few days. Each day, encourage your child to say and spell the words out loud.

Numbers reinforce the concept that letters in words are in a specific sequence.

4. **Dry-erase Writing Practice** – Wal-Mart and other discount stores carry many materials for pre-readers and beginning readers. Look in the school supplies section of the store. Look for a dry-erase tablet that features the letters of the alphabet with arrows within each letter that show the child where to start when printing out a specific letter of the alphabet and which way to move the pencil as he is making that letter. Once you've purchased one of these tablets, spend a few minutes a day (or even a few minutes each week if you can't make time for this every day), helping your child learn to print each of the letters of the alphabet on this dry-erase tablet. Spending time with your child to do this, rather than simply telling him to go do this alone, will further reinforce that you feel learning to recognize and print the letters of the alphabet are important skills you can't wait for your child to acquire.

5. **Alphabet Card Practice** – Purchase two sets of alphabet cards. These are usually available at

discount stores like Wal-Mart and Target. Alphabet cards with colorful pictures – which represent each letter's initial sound – are eye appealing. Plus, pictures help children attach meaning to each letter name. Tack up one set of cards at your child's eye level on a wall. A kitchen wall is good place. Meal times are not only a good time to develop your children's conversational skills but also a good time to introduce and review previously learned letter names.

Note, if you're a preschool teacher, place these cards under the chalkboard in your classroom. Young children often have undiagnosed vision problems. Placing alphabet cards under the blackboard like this ensures each child will seem them clearly.

Begin teaching each letter by saying its name. For example, "this is the letter "D", the word dog starts with "D". Introduce just 7 letters at a time. Have your child or student say each letter name and practice writing it. Have a pre-made sheet created of each letter name for your children or students to trace over several times (if you're working at home with your own child, the dry-erase tablet suggested in the previous activity is perfect for this).

After seven letters have been taught, assess your child or students to see if they know each letter name. Simply place the seven alphabet cards in front of them and ask them to identify each letter name. If they know all seven move onto another set of seven. If there were letter names they could not identify, keep them in a separate pile so you can reintroduce these letters with a new set of seven letters.

Repeat this process of introducing 7 letters at a time until your child or students master the names of all the letters of the alphabet.

6. **Picture Phone Book** – Create a picture phone book with your child. Gather photographs of family members. Paste a photo of each person in the phone book.

Next to the photo, have the child print out that person's phone number. Additionally, (if you think your child is ready for this and won't call 911 when there is no emergency), have the child print 911 for emergency (with a photo of an emergency), but explain to your child that this number is to ONLY be used by the child if a parent or other adult can't make the call.

7. **Word Wall** – Make a word wall for your child. Once your child has learned a few simple words, print each word on a separate index card. Tack up the cards on a bulletin board that is used exclusively as your child's word wall. Encourage your child to use his words in speech and in writing, and to look for, and identify, his words in books you read to him. You'll probably be amazed and pleasantly surprised at how your child or student takes "ownership" for these words and quickly points them out each time they appear in text you read together. "The process of copying new words strengthens student's memory for those words and does so rather enduringly (Adam, p102)."

8. **Zoo Trip**

Plan a trip to the zoo with your child. You might already enjoy visiting the zoo with your child, but here's how to make it an activity that will help your child get ready to read. Before you go, get a picture book from the library that features zoo animals. Read the book aloud to your child and have her repeat the names of all the animals in the book. Take the book with you when you go to the zoo. When you see a monkey at the zoo, open the book to the page of the monkey and point it out to your child. This will help your child begin to see the connection between words, pictures, and actual events, objects, etc.

"The more prior knowledge you have about a topic the easier it is to understand what a story is about or subject matter in a textbook."
(Teaching in the 21st Century)

10. Finger Puppets
Make finger puppets to go with a story. Cut the fingers off some old gloves and use fabric markers to draw the characters on the socks together. You can also roll felt or paper for the body and glue eyes, noses, smiles, and hair on them. Note: To create patterns for the characters, make color copies from the book that features these characters. Cut out the characters' faces, and glue them onto the glove fingers or rolled paper or felt. Once you make the puppets, your child can use them to help tell the story as you read it from the book.

11. **Books on Tape or CD** – Listen to books on tape or CD together. You can check out tapes and

CDs from the library for free or buy them at a bookstore (to save money, stop by your local used bookstore. Kids love listening while someone else reads them a story—while they follow along in their own books. Also use the tapes at bedtime. Let the child select his favorite tape as a bedtime story.

12. Family Reading Time

Set a family reading time. For 15 or 20 minutes a night, everyone in the house reads a story together. If friends or neighbors are visiting, ask them to participate. Show your child that reading is fun for the whole family.

Making Your Home or Classroom a More Reader Friendly Space

The expression "reader friendly space" describes a home or classroom where reading, writing and speaking are promoted and nurtured. Reader friendly homes and classrooms have bookshelves full of books and displays of books on tables and counter tops. Displays like this provides children with a variety of reading choices, encourages and supports reading growth. Literate homes and classrooms that celebrate books set aside time every day to practice reading.

Suggestions for parents and teachers who want to create reader friendly spaces:

> **Model:** One of the most important things parents and teachers can do, is read aloud. This demonstrates to children then enjoyment of reading. When adults model the pleasures of reading, children naturally value and emulate reading themselves.

- **Time:** Children must practice reading every day in order to become successful readers. For homes and classrooms to be literate rich environments, reading time needs to be scheduled every day.

- **Classroom:** Teachers need to provide a variety of reading materials to encourage their students to read. Provide a selection of picture books, books on poetry, humorous fiction, and non-fiction texts on social studies, science, and even comic books. All should be available for students to explore and read.

- **Home:** Besides providing a variety of books parents need to show an interest in their child's reading growth. Take time to look over reading worksheets completed at school and praise your child for his good work. Most importantly, make a point to read aloud to your child. Make an effort to take your child to libraries and bookstores.

Also, give your child books for gifts, as often as you can. Reading is a lifelong skill everyone needs. When parents and teachers create homes and classrooms areas full of books, children experience success and enjoyment happens, as they learn to read.

SUGGESTED BOOKS FOR PRE-READERS

12 of the Best Books for Babies and Toddlers

Fortunately, there are thousands of wonderful books for babies and toddlers on the market today. Here are just a dozen to enjoy with your children or students. Many of these books are available at your local library or bookstore. Almost all of them can be purchased online at amazon.com.

1.   Chicka Chicka Boom Boom by Bill Martin Jr. and John Archambault, illustrated by Lois Ehlert. Letters of the alphabet race each other to the top of the coconut tree in this story told in lively rhyme.

2.   Baby Faces by Margaret Miller. Babies love this book that features the faces of other babies.

3.   What A Baby series of board books by Cheryl Willis Hudson, illustrated by George Ford. Simple concept books that feature realistic illustrations of cute African-American

4.   Baby Cakes by Karma Wilson, illustrated by Sam Williams. A cute interactive board

book that is perfect for babies and toddlers. The catchy rhymes help children learn to recognize language patterns.

5. Caps For Sale by Esphyr Slobodkina. A peddler who goes from town to town with all his wares (caps) on his head falls asleep under a tree. Some monkeys take his caps and the peddler must outsmart them in order to get his caps back. Children love this story because they know what the monkeys are doing LONG before the peddler does!

6. Frances by Russell Hoban. Charming series of picture books that features a precocious and spirited little badger named Frances.

7. Wheels of The Bus by Raffi. As a rickety old bus collects a strange assortment of passengers in a quaint little town, the reader may join in with the sounds of the bus and motions of the driver and passengers.

8. Where the Wild Things Are by Maurice Sendak. The book tells the story of Max, who one evening plays around his home making "mischief" in a wolf costume. As

punishment, his mother sends him to bed without supper. In his room, a mysterious, wild forest and sea grows out of his imagination, and Max sails to the land of the Wild.

9.   Horton Hears Who by Dr. Seuss. The story of Horton the elephant who, on the afternoon of May 15 while splashing in a pool located in the Jungle of Nool, hears a small speck of dust talking to him. Horton discovers that the speck of dust is actually a tiny planet, home to a microscopic community called Whoville, where the Whos reside. The Whos are led by a character known as the Mayor.

10.   I Wonder Why Camels Have Humps and Other Questions About Animals by Anita Ganeri. This book is packed with some of the questions children most often ask about animals, such as, "Why do leopards have spots?" and "Why can't penquins fly?" and "How many ants can an anteater eat?"

11.   Read-Aloud Rhymes for the Very Young edited by Jack Prelutsky. This poetry anthology for children has been around for

a while, but it's still perfect for today's young children. The poems included in this volume are by 119 of the best-known poets of the 20th century.

12. <u>Favorite Nursery Rhymes From Mother Goose</u> by Scott Gustafson. The illustrations and rhymes in this volume will entertain children and adults alike.

The Importance of Nursery Rhymes

Songs and rhymes for young children have been passed down for generations. They are fun, children love them, and they provide a warm, nurturing experience between parent and child. What parents may not realize, as they recite simple nursery rhymes or sing songs with their children is nursery rhymes have important educational value.

"Experts in literacy and child development have discovered that if children know eight nursery thymes by heart by the time they're four years old, they're usually among the best readers by the time they're eight." (Fox, M. 2001)
Sources Reading Magic, San Diego, CA; Harcourt.
www.kbyueleven.org

ADDITIONAL RESOURCES FOR PRE-READERS

12 More Great Resources for Pre-readers, including Websites, Software, Games, Puzzles

Books are not the only great resources for helping young children get ready to read. Here are some popular software programs, games, puzzles, and websites that can help you help your children or students at the pre-reading stage.

1. Hooked ON Phonics Pre-K *Programs* for ages 3-4. These are great for helping children get ready to read by learning rhyming, beginning sounds, and letter name and sounds. Each program includes a DVD, workbook, and short books your child can actually read after they've been through several lessons.

2. Learn to Read This program includes the entire kindergarten to 3rd grade phonics curriculum taught at USA public schools. It includes 100 interactive cartoon animated online phonics lessons in a game-like environment that is fun and easy to use.

3. www.Click'nKids.com Click 'n Read Spelling (for PreK through 5th grade). Teaches the 800 most commonly used words in the English language.

4. Magnetic Refrigerator Magnets Leapfrog Fridge Phonics Teaching letters sing lovely learning songs. Your child can arrange the letters however she wants and will acquire advanced motor skills and develop better letter recognition. Available at Target and other discount stores. As well as, online.

5. Think Fun What's Gnu A three-letter learning game for children ages three to five. An inexpensive and fun game that teaches children "letter word families" and how to blend sounds into words. Several children can play this game together, so it's perfect for the classroom.

6. www.zerotothree.com is a non-profit dedicated to the development and well-being of infants and toddlers. In their "Behavior & Development" section on their website, they address Early Language and Literacy, offering informational articles and suggestions for activities.

7. www.earlyliteracylearning.org *The Center for Early Literacy Learning* (CELL) draws from research across the country to provide information and activities in their guides for parents.

8. www.nectac.com *NECTAC*, the National Early Childhood Technical Assistance Center is a government center that produces research and information on developing language and early literacy skills. Visit the website for fun activities for word building, rhyming, vocabulary development, and more!

9. Leap Frog Talking Words Factory for ages 2-5. Leap Frog characters (Leap, Lily, and Tad) come to life in this fun DVD, where the Word Whammer, Sticky-Ick-O-Rama, and more amazing machines take letters and make them into words! Includes humorous songs too.

10. www.samsoncsclassroom.com Computer software developed for kindergarteners to first graders to help them learn, memorize and instantly recognize common sight words, such as: the, is to, then.

11. <u>Reader Rabbit - Learn to Read Phonics</u>
Kids love Reader Rabbit. In this program features more than 100 interactive games and puzzles, printable arts and crafts activities, and 10 irresistible songs that play on your computer or on any CD player. Also includes four extra game activities that reinforce essential skills.

12. <u>Let's Get Ready For Kindergarten</u> *Let's Get Ready for Kindergarten!* and, *Let's Get Ready for First Grade!* Two wonderfully helpful books from Cedar Valley Publishing that helps parents and kids prepare for kindergarten and first grade. Find out what your child is expected to know even BEFORE he starts school so he will be prepared!

PART TWO

FOR BEGINNING READERS
Preschoolers – Second Graders

Learning to read is exciting for children. Preschool age children are fascinated with books. They delight in turning the pages, pointing out colorful illustrations of animals and children their own age, while learning about the world that surrounds them by way of enchanting stories.

Once children start attending kindergarten they begin learning letters of the alphabet and their corresponding sounds. They are also introduced to blending letter sounds into short words. Short stories about objects they are familiar with – in sentences that are no more than five to seven words long – are their first reading books.

Additionally, a number of "sight" words are taught such as: can, the, it, saw, where, what, that, etc. These words are most often used in sentences and ones children need to memorize and recognize instantly.

By the first grade children are introduced to vowel and consonant combinations such as, oo, ea, ch, sh, etc. Instruction in blending sounds into words continues. Children are now reading stories that are a little longer. But they should not be expected to read them perfectly, again about topics and objects familiar to them in everyday life. More "sight" words are taught, and need to be memorized.

In the second grade, additional reading concepts in our written language are taught — prefixes, suffices, etc. Again, stories are longer and students should not be expected to read these stories perfectly. Also, about objects familiar to them in everyday life, while also introducing unfamiliar concepts and topics

READING MILESTONES FOR BEGINNING READERS

Pre-School Milestones/Expectations

Children in preschool should be able to recall nursery rhymes and verses, and recognize rhymes when they hear them. As well, they should understand print concepts in books such as, what is the cover of the book, a page of a book, and that pages are turned from left to right.

Kindergarten Milestones/Expectations – End Of The Year

By the end of kindergarten children should know all the letters and sounds of the alphabet. Know a number of sight-words and are able to read four to eight word sentences. Understand that a story has a beginning, middle, end, main character and be able to recount what a particular story was about. As well as, count sounds in words, clap syllables and provide a rhyming word for a given word.

First Grade Milestones/Expectations – End Of The Year

Once children have passed through the first grade they should know how printed words are organized –

words, sentences, paragraphs. Be aware of punctuation and grammar. Read (with 70% accuracy) the reading literature book, provided by the school district and recognize all the sight words they have been taught. As well as, possess the ability to blend sounds into words, while also sounding out unknown words while they read them.

Second Grade Milestones/Expectations – End of The Year

Children should possess a comprehensive knowledge of phonics elements (consonants, vowels, blends, syllables, common phonics rules). Be able to blend three to four sounds (when spoken aloud) into to words. Possess the ability to sound unknown words out. Students should know how to break longer words into three syllables or more, as well as, to read their literature book at 70% accuracy when reading.

How to Read Aloud to Children

Reading a story aloud to your children or students may seem like a straightforward activity. However, including the following critical steps reveals to children why reading is enjoyable, teaches them specific elements found in stories, while helping them develop good story comprehension.

Follow these easy steps to help kids get the most out of reading aloud time, at school or home:

- **Preview:** Talk about the cover of the book. Point out the colorful illustration on the cover of the book.

- **Activate Background Knowledge:** Discuss with your children and students what they might already know about the story. For example, if the story is about a dog or a bear have children share knowledge they already have about these animals. When children attach what they already know about a topic, this helps them learn about new topics and concepts.

- **Predictions:** Flip through the story's pages prior to reading. Point out the colorful illustration within the story. Ask your children or students what they think the story will be about. Next, ask your children or students to make predictions about what they think the story is going to be about—based on the story's illustrations. This helps children interact intellectually with what they're reading – no guessing.

- **Pacing:** Don't Rush! Read aloud slowly. Before turning each page discuss what's going on in the story so far. Such as: "what's going on in the story so far," "who is (are) the main character(s)", and "where does this story take place". Again, ask for predictions, based on what has been read so far (no guessing) about what may happen next in the story. Checking predictions while reading helps children monitor their understanding of what's being read. Also, reading slowly gives children time to think about what's going on in the story.

- **Pointing:** As you read aloud place your finger under each word as you say it. This helps children develop written word recognition, while also helping them associate the story's words to the illustrations on each page of the book.

- **Posing Questions:** After reading the story with your children or students pose discussion questions. Such as, "did the story end the way everyone expected it to", "what new knowledge was learned", "what part of the story did the class, or children like best about the story?" Summarizing new knowledge helps children hold onto to new concepts taught.

- **Paper and Pencil:** Have your students or children write a two to three page reflection on the story. Reading and writing development are directly connected. Writing activities after reading helps children develop vocabulary and improves automatic word recognition.

Taking time out of each day, or reading aloud at least once a week is one of the most important activities that help children learn how to read.

"The single most important activity for building knowledge required for eventual reading success in reading is reading aloud to children." (Becoming a Nation of Readers — The Report of the Commission On Reading 1985)

ACTIVITIES FOR BEGINNING READERS

12 Popular Games, Puzzles, and Other Activities for Beginning Readers

Again, the main point for parents and teachers of children who are just beginning to read is to help children enjoy reading. Here are a dozen activities, puzzles, and games, etc. to try together.

1. Alphabet Bingo – This is a fun activity parents and teachers can enjoy with their own children or students, to help them memorize each letter of the alphabet.

Here's what you'll need:

White Construction Paper – Create a grid of squares on the sheet of construction paper. Make sure you have 26 squares. You may end up with more squares; depending on how many rows you draw horizontally, and vertically.

Black Marker – Randomly write each letter of the alphabet on each square. Repeat letters in additional squares.

Note: Make sure you write out each letter uniformly. Alphabet letters/symbols should look exactly like the letter cards you are going to show (while you're playing Alphabet Bingo). Remember, learning the symbols that represent each letter of the alphabet is the goal of this game. Uniformity and clarity are critical.

Plastic Dots – These will be used to place on the squares as alphabet letters are called out. Pennies or buttons work too.

Alphabet Cards – Buy a deck of alphabet letter cards.

Alphabet cards are very inexpensive. They can be purchased in both bookstores and teacher supply stores.

Here's how to play the game:

Begin playing Alphabet Bingo by saying aloud the alphabet letter name, then holding up the card so it can be seen clearly. Direct your child or student(s) to match the alphabet letter card, you are holding up, with the alphabet letter written on their construction paper grid. Next, direct them to place a dot, penny or bead on the square, to cover that letter.

After playing Alphabet Bingo time after time, you will notice that your child or student(s) start to memorize each letter name. Soon, they won't need the letter cards to remind them of the letter names, when they hear them.

Hint: Parents should consider repeating the letters of your child's name in the additional spaces. As far as how you want to reward your child, or students for recognizing and matching each letter correctly, is up to you. There are many version of traditional bingo. With your child and students in mind, decide how you want to reward their progress.

"The single best prediction of students' end-of-year reading achievement — regardless of instructional approaches — was their ability at the beginning of the year to recognize and name upper and lower case letters." (Adams, p.10, 1986)

2. **Mail Call** – Make a "mailbox" out of a shoebox or clean milk carton. Place the box on a low counter or table where your child can easily reach

it. During the day, leave notes, cards, letters, etc. for your child in this mailbox.

Classroom teachers, use cubbies as mailboxes. Let each child "post" one letter a day to someone else in the class. You can match each child in the class with another who will be his/her "pen pal" or let the children choose their own pen pals. Make letter writing and "mail call" a regular part of the day.

3. **Alphabet poster** – Ask your child to draw each letter of the alphabet on some poster board, then go through magazines and catalogs and help your child cut out pictures of things that begin with each letter and glue them on the board. This is a great hands-on way to learn the alphabet.

4. **Reading Journal** – Have your child keep a reading journal listing every book she reads. Next, suggest that your child draw a picture to illustrate something she learned from each book whenever she makes an entry in the journal, along with the name of the book and date read.

5. **Fairy Tales** – Help your child create his own fairy tale by cutting pictures out of magazines. Have him look for pictures of the following:

- A person or animal who will be the main character
- A place that will be the setting for the story
- Another person or animal who looks like trouble and will be the villain or antagonist
- A place that represents where the main character will live "happily ever after."

The pictures should be glued onto construction paper – one picture per page – to make a picture book.

After the child has found each of the pictures and glued all them to the pages of construction paper, have him use the pictures to tell you his story as you write it down.

6. **Place Cards** – Have your child make place cards for each member of your family for a special meal. Print out the names of each person who will be at the table on a sheet of paper. Cut out small pieces of poster-board or tag-board to use for the place cards. Have your child write

each person's name on a place card using a colorful marker. Colorful stickers can be added to the place cards to decoration.

7. **Sing-alongs** – Post the lyrics to a simple song on piece of paper on the wall or write them on a chalkboard and encourage the children to sing along to a record, CD, or tape.

8. **Reading Log** – Once your child is reading simple books on her own, have her create a reading log, where she records the title of the book she is reading, then set an amount of time each day for her to read her book (not too long; just 10 to 15 minutes). At the end of that time, have the child write down in her reading log, the numbers of the pages she read that day.

Note: You can create your own reading log and read a book when your child is reading. Then record how many pages you read each day. At the end of each reading session, talk with your child about the book you read. Ask questions about the book she read.

9. **Mental Pictures** – Read a short picture book, like Where the Wild Things Are by Maurice Sendak, aloud to your children or students. Tell them you are not going to show them the pictures in the book as you read. Instead, you want them to create pictures of the characters in their minds. Explain to the children that by creating their own mental pictures of the characters, the place where the story happens, and what the characters are doing can actually help them enjoy and understand the story better.

Note: If you'd like, after you've read the story without showing children the illustrations, show them the illustrations and have them talk about how these pictures are the alike or different from their mental pictures.

10. **Picture Dictionaries** – Have your child or students make picture dictionaries. Write each of the letters of the alphabet on the chalkboard then have the children tell you several items that begin with each letter so you can write these words under the appropriate letters. Once you have several words listed for each letter of the alphabet, pass out some magazines and have the

children look for pictures of these words. They can use safety scissors to cut out the pictures.

Then have the children glue the pictures to construction paper – one piece of paper for each letter of the alphabet, with each letter printed at the top of the page. Once the children have found pictures for all the letters and have pasted them to the pieces of construction paper, you can either staple the pages together for them to make a book, or punch holes in the pages and give the children pieces of yarn they can lace through the holes and tie them together to make their books.

Note: This activity should take place over several days. Have children look for pictures for just one or two letters during a single session.

11. **Flash Card Spelling Bee** – Use alphabet flash cards for a spelling bee. Hold up a card and have the child tell you the letter on the card. If the child tells you the correct letter, continue with all the letters in the card deck.

12. **Give Directions** – Have each child explain how to do something (how to feed a baby, how to get ready for bed, etc., something the child

obviously knows how to do). Giving directions for how to do something helps children learn sequencing and communicating skills, which are important in reading and writing.

The Importance of Rhyming in Early Reading Development

When young children are read nursery rhymes this is their first introduction to rhyming words. Stories told in rhyme help children learn how to distinguish individual sounds within words. Researchers in early reading development observed children age three to school age. They found that reading nursery rhymes to children who are learning to read, contributed to later reading success.

SUGGESTED BOOKS FOR BEGINNING READERS

12 Popular Books for Children Just Beginning to Read

Fortunately, there are thousands of wonderful books for beginning readers on the market, and new ones are being published all the time. Here is a list that will help you and your child develop some favorites you enjoy reading over and over again together.

1. Four Fur Feet by Margaret Wise Brown. Illustrated by Woodleigh Marx Hubbard. Told in **rhyme**, this story features a furry little creature that travels the world, making note of all the sights and sounds.

2. Mary Wore Her Red Dress by Merle Peek. On Katy's birthday, all of her animal friends come to the party dressed in clothes of different colors.

3. The Cat Sat on The Mat by Alice Cameron. Illustrated by Carol Jones. Visual gags about a cat who must be the center of attention.

4. The Little Red Hen by Margot Zemach.

This classic tale tells the story of a little red hen who gets no help at all from her friends when it's time to plant, harvest, or prepare some wheat into bread, so she does it all (even eats the bread) herself.

5. Three Little Fish by Frank Asch. The concept of opposites, such as little and big, is explored through pages that fold out.

6. Shhhh by Kevin Henkes. Someone wakes up and quietly moves around the house while everyone else is still sleeping.

7. Follow The Leader by Miela Ford. A sequel to Ford's *Bear Play*. Features large, clear photographs of playful polar bear cubs with short, simple sentences as captions in bold type. Uses many common "sight words" and clues to unfamiliar words in the text.

8. Black dog Red House by Lizi Boyd. Introduces toddlers and pre-schoolers to colors in a fun and engaging way.

9. I See something You Don't See by Robin Michal Koontz. Two children try to pass the time at Grandma's by playing a popular guessing game that readers can participate in.

10. <u>Little Bear</u> by Diane Namm. Illustrated by Lisa McCue. Young children wiil love learning to read with these storybooks. Once they can recognize and identify the words used to tell each story, they will be able to successfully read on their own. Features a word list.

11. <u>Shoelaces</u> by Suzanne Lieurance Illustrated by Patrick Girouard. This book is part of the Rookie Readers series of beginning readers. Each book in the series actively engages young readers, encouraging language development, building fluency, and promoting independent reading. In this one, written in rhyme, a little girl and her dog show off her collection of shoelaces.

12. <u>Henry and Mudge</u> *The First Book* by Cynthia Rylant. Illustrated by Suçie Stevenson. A series about an only child and his huge best friend, a mastiff named Mudge.

ADDITIONAL RESOURCES FOR BEGINNING READERS

12 More Great Resources for Beginning Readers, including Websites, Software, Games, Puzzles

The following websites, software, and games will give you plenty of resources to help your beginning reader.

1. www.starfall.com Learn to Read with Phonics. A free website to teach children to read with phonics. For preschool, kindergarten, and first grade. Includes phonics games and online interactive books.

2. www.crickweb.co.uk Free online education resources and games.

3. Dolch Basic Words List Use the list to make flashcards, bingo games, or matching games to help your child learn these basic words.

4. Jumpstart Phonics JumpStart skill-building workbooks help children become better and confident readers. Kids Learn: sound recognition, letter recognition, word building, rhyming, spelling, vocabulary words,

consonants, vowels, blends, and more.

5. Jumpstart Phonics Read and Rhyme This is a step-by-step system that helps children learn to read. JumpStart Phonics is an integrated learning system that teaches essential phonics skills – the building blocks of reading, with Voice-Recognition technology. Children play fun learning games and receive immediate feedback as they hear, see and speak phonetic sounds.

5. www.spencerlearning.com Phonics lessons for beginning, intermediate and struggling readers, as well as lessons for advanced readers.

7. Clifford the Big Red Dog Learning Activities The software teaches important reading skills like letter patterns.

8. Bailey's Book House Teaches beginning reading skills to young children.

9. What's Gnu A great way for younger players to practice their word recognition and spelling skills, this game is a fun confidence-builder. Players slide the "Letter Getter" forward to reveal two letter tiles, and then use them to

create three-letter words by filling in the blanks on their Word-Starter cards.

10. <u>Word Munchers</u> An educational way to build confidence in reading! Muncher program utilizes an engaging 3D animated game board; as students practice word identification, sentence completion, and rhyme.

11. <u>Let's Learn Sight Words</u> Fun and engaging videos to explore Fry's first 100 sight words, including using the words in context.

12. <u>Games for Reading From Doctor Suess</u> Laugh while learning basic reading skills. Designed to teach basic reading skills, Dr. Seuss Reading Games Software brings two of your favorite Dr. Seuss titles to life. Designed for beginners, Dr. Seuss ABC introduces children to the ABCs of reading. Learn the ABCs by singing and memorizing the alphabet song. In the ever-popular Cat In The Hat, games and activities appear on every page. Click on a noun to see a picture, or click on a verb to see an action. Kids learn more than 600 words as they play.

PART THREE

FOR INTERMEDIATE READERS
Third Graders - Sixth Graders

By the third grade, children should be reading to learn subject matter taught in school. Instruction in phonics, learning how to manipulate sounds into words, has typically ended, although there are lessons in English literature, in a variety of forms of fiction and non-fiction that continue. By the third grade, children are expected to be accomplished readers who are capable of reading their social studies, science, math, and language arts textbooks.

Reading Milestones For Intermediate Readers

Children in grades third through sixth should be able to read textbooks and other non-fiction formats accurately and with understanding. Be aware of other forms of literature, such as, fictional stories, poetry, folktales, biography, etc., and have a good knowledge of phonics rules and be able to blend sounds within unknown words.

"There's a misconception today America's children cannot read. To the contrary, children in America can read, although many encounter reading formats they are unfamiliar with. So, parents and teachers need to provide home and school opportunities to expose their children and students to these other kinds of reading."
(Becoming a Nation of Readers, 1985)

Informational Formats – What Children Need to Learn

Students early on learn stories have a: setting, characters, problem and resolution. However, when students are presented with textbook passages, those that expose information rather than tell a story, they often have difficulty understanding what they're reading.

Here are three kinds of informational formats with which students need to become familiar:

- **Essays** - An essay is usually structured in five main parts. The introductory paragraph, two to three supporting paragraphs, and a closing paragraph that summarizes the information in the essay.

- **Science, Social Studies, and Mathematics Textbooks** – Subject matter books such as these use both words and graphics to expose information, while sometimes introducing subject matter in a sequential format. Students need to learn how to retain sequences of information and learn to look for facts identified in graphs, sidebars, charts, etc.

- **Newspapers** – Articles in newspapers are organized in order of importance. There is a lead paragraph followed by important details supplemented with answers to who, what, where, when and why.

ACTIVITIES FOR INTERMEDIATE READERS

12 Games, Puzzles, and Other Activities for 3rd Through 6th Graders Who Are Reading at Grade Level

Since intermediate readers are now reading to learn instead of simply learning to read, the games, puzzles, and other activities listed here will develop critical thinking skills, which are important if children are to become skillful readers.

1. **Origami** – the Japanese art of folding paper. Not only is Origami fun, it teachers students/children how to follow step-by-step written instruction, as well. Making Origami figures also reinforces another important concept. Children learn when they miss or skip steps that not only does their Origami project come out incorrectly but the same will be true about other assignments or activities, which also require sequential steps.

Schedule about thirty minutes of time to read about Origami. Then, with your child or class, make animals, birds, boxes and other shapes in colorful Origami paper. This is a great activity for reluctant readers. Why? Origami is a hands-on activity. These readers are now motivated to read in order to complete and finish their Origami figures. Origami fills the learning needs of children who learn quickly and like challenging projects, too, since Origami figures can be very simple, yet even quite complicated, to make.

2. **Role Playing** – Have children act out a play. There are many Readers Theater scripts that feature easy to read dialogue with parts for several children. Put the words "Readers Theater" in an online search engine to get lists of many books in this genre.

3. **Paired Reading** – Sometimes referred to as buddy reading, this is an activity any parent can do with his or her child. It's really quite simple. The parent (the more capable reader) reads aloud, while the child (the less capable reader), follows along. Variations of paired reading are when both the parent and child read the same passage aloud together, or when the parent and child take turns reading parts of a story or other text aloud (the parent reads a page, then the child reads the next

page, for example). Paired Reading is a good activity to help children develop comprehension skills because, while the parent is reading (doing the work of decoding and identifying words), the child can focus on comprehension – understanding what's going on in the story.

First, select a book at your child's instructional level. This means a book your child can read, but has not mastered– a book your child cannot read with fluency. For example, if your child is in the early elementary grades and reading at that level, the Magic Tree House Boxed Set, Books 1-4: Dinosaurs Before Dark, The Knight at Dawn, Mummies in the Morning, and Pirates Past Noon would be a good choice of books you can read together.

If your child is in middle school (and reading at this level), a wonderful book to pair read together is My Side of the Mountain.

Follow these steps for Paired Reading:

- Preview the book with your child. Look at any visual clues such as illustrations or to what the book will be about.

- Set a purpose for reading. Encourage your child to make predictions about what is going to be read. A good prompt is, "after seeing the pictures what do you think this stories going to be about"? Have your child predict, then read a short passage or a page and verify his predictions, then read another page, etc., repeating this process all the way through the story.

- Make sure your child follows along with his finger under each word being read. Seeing words while simultaneously hearing them helps children develop sight word vocabulary.

- Read aloud, with accuracy and feeling when it's your turn to read. Encourage your child to do this, too.

- Preview the book with your child. Look at any visual clues such as illustrations or chapter headings that give the child ideas as to what the book will be about.

This reading activity not only helps children to become more confident readers, but it helps them learn to enjoy reading.

Reading Comprehension Activity

Learning the alphabet, its corresponding sounds, and how to blend letter sounds into words, is just one aspect of becoming a capable reader—the ability to understand words in sentences is the goal of every reading endeavor.

Reading comprehension activities are developed to teach students how to monitor their own reading. Specifically, children focus on individual sentences and chunks of texts as they move through a selection of passages.

The following sequence of steps is a reading comprehension strategy. Each step is designed to help children learn how to:

- Focus on what they're reading,

- Develop the ability to monitor and recognize when they comprehend or do not comprehend.

- Learn to re-read misunderstood passages and re-read them again for understanding.

- Subsequently, achieve meaning of both narrative and textbook materials they read.

Step 1. Talk about the topic that is going to be read. This allows children to attach what they already know about a particular topic to what they're about to read.

Step 2. Pre-teach vocabulary. Preview the text prior to assigning the reading lesson. Identify words you may think your children may be unfamiliar with. Define each word and give examples of their use in real-life situations.

Step 3. Preview the story or text. Based on the chapter titles or sub-titles have your children make a prediction(s) about what they are going to be reading about.

Step 4. Read the first few paragraphs. Clarify whether any predictions were confirmed or denied.

Step 5. Talk about what has been learned so far. Make new predictions based upon what has been read so far if necessary.

Step 6. Repeat steps one through five until the end of the assigned reading.

This reading comprehension activity teaches children how to activate their prior knowledge, make predictions then confirm predictions, while pre-teaching vocabulary. All critical steps needed in order for children to learn how to understand stories and textbook passages.

4. **Reading journal** – Reading and writing are intertwined. Research shows that children who write about what they've read become better readers and writers, so have your child keep a reading journal.

The best way to get your child to begin connecting reading and writing is to have her start a daily, reading journal. Getting started is really quite easy. Just buy your child an inexpensive spiral notebook or use a three-ring notebook with notebook paper. As the days and months pass, you will notice your child is expanding her listening and written vocabularies through journaling. She is also learning the mechanics of writing, including punctuation, grammar and spelling. Daily journaling also helps children become more comfortable and confident about reading and writing.

5. **Shared Story Telling** – Alternate telling a story that your child/students already know well. You start the story. Stop after a few scenes of the story and ask your child to tell what

happened next. To try this activity with a class, let each child tell one scene of the story.

6. **Letter Writing** – Have children write letters to their favorite character in a book. Classroom teachers can divide the class into pairs and have each pair of students take on the roles of two characters in the same book. For example, one student might take on the role of the protagonist in a book, the other student in that pair would take on the role of the antagonist. The two students in each pair can write letters to each other as their characters.

7. **Series Books** – Encourage your child to read books in a series. Help your child find a genre that interests him. You may to introduce the concept of "genre" and give examples of various genre series. Once your child has found a genre and a series within that genre that he likes, encourage him to read each book in the series. Series reading can be used in conjunction with other activities listed here, such as paired reading or keeping a reading journal.

8. **Greeting Cards** – Have children make greeting cards from construction paper, colored markers, stickers, etc. and give the cards to friends and family members. This is another activity that helps children see the connection between reading and writing. You might go to the bookstore or other store that sells greeting cards and look at several cards with your child to help him get some ideas as to what kind of text to include in a greeting card.

9. **Invitations** – Have children write their own invitations to parties and other events. Before you child begins, discuss what kinds of information need to be included on an invitation.

As your child acquires keyboarding skills, he can create cards using the computer, then print the cards out on your printer.

10. **Nature Discussion** – Being literate means more than just able to read and write. It also means learning to talk about what we read and experience. Take your child on a walk through the neighborhood or a nearby park. Talk to your

child about what you are seeing, hearing, smelling, and touching. When you get back home, sit down with your child and together write about your walk.

11. **Recorded Readings** – Have your child read aloud into a tape recorder and listen to the recording to check for fluency. Make tape recorded readings part of your child's regular reading practice at home.

12. **Magazine Subscriptions** – Get a subscription in his or her name to an age-appropriate magazine or two. Encourage your child to read the magazine(s) on his own each time a new issue arrives, then ask him to tell you what he read.

SUGGESTED BOOKS FOR INTERMEDIATE READERS

12 Popular or Classic Books for 3rd Through 6th Graders Who Are Reading at Grade Level

Your child may read some of these books as part of his regular school assignments. But, if he doesn't, it's a good idea to introduce these wonderful books to him.

1. Island of The Blue Dolphins by Scott O'Dell. A young girl is stranded for years on an island off the California coast. Based on the true story of Juana Maria, a Nicoleño Indian left alone for 18 years on San Nicolas Island in the 19th century.

2. Indian in The Cupboard by Lynn Reid Banks. A plastic miniature Indian that magically comes to life into a mysterious old cupboard changes a young man's life.

3. Shiloh by Phyllis Reynolds Naylor. Marty Preston comes across a young beagle in the hills behind his home. He learns that the dog's name is Shiloh, and he belongs to Judd Travers, who drinks too much, has a gun, and isn't nice to

his dogs. When Shiloh runs away to Marty, big trouble starts.

4.   Robots of Dawn by Isaac Asimov. A futuristic story of the unlikely partnership between a New York City detective and a humanoid robot who must learn to work together.

5.   Tales of a Fourth Grade Nothing by Judy Blume. Peter Hatcher feels like a fourth grade nothing. His little brother Fudge is causing problems for him all the time. Fudge gets away with everything. The last straw is when Fudge walks off with Peter's pet turtle, Dribble. Peter must get his parents to pay attention to him for a change.

6.   Superfudge by Judy Blume. Peter is a sixth grade student who lives in New York City. He has a little brother, fondly known as Fudge. Peter's mom informs him that she is going to be having another baby. Peter worries the new baby will create the same problems for him as fudge, and he plans to run away. More big new follows when Peter's parents decide to move the family from the big city, to the suburbs in Princeton, New Jersey.

7. <u>Harriet The Spy</u> by Louise Fitzhugh. Harriet M. Welsch is a spy. In her notebook, she writes down everything she knows about everyone, even her classmates and her best friends. Then Harriet loses track of her notebook, and it ends up in the wrong hands. Before she can stop them, her friends have read the things she's written about each of them and no longer want to be her friends, so she has to find a way to rebuild her friendships.

8. <u>From The Mixed Up Files of Mrs. Basil Frankenweiler</u> by E. L. Konigsburg. Claudia Kincaid decides to run away to a place that is comfortable, beautiful, and preferably elegant – the Metropolitan Museum of Art in New York City. But she has a cash flow problem, so she invites her brother Jamie along since he has money. Claudia and Jamie find themselves caught up in a mystery involving an angel statue that might be worth millions even though the museum purchased it at an auction for just $250. The mystery leads Claudia to Mrs. Basil E. Frankweiler, the remarkable old woman who sold the statue.

9. <u>A Rat's Tale</u> by Tor Seidler. Young Montague Mad-Rat lives in under New York City. But he knows very few rats besides his mother, his father, and his Aunt Elizabeth. But his life takes a quick turn when he meets Isabel Moberly-Rat on his way home from Central Park.

10. <u>The Nose From Jupiter</u> by Richard Scrimger. Alan Dingwall isn't strong or good at soccer or math and other kids bully him. But when Norbert, an alien from Jupiter, comes to earth on an exploration mission and moves into Alan's nose, Alan changes.

11. <u>The Golden Pathway</u> by Donna McDine. David, befriends Jenkins, the slave owned by David's Pa. David leads Jenkins to freedom with no regard for his own safety or the possible consequences from Pa.

12. <u>The Magic Treehouse Series</u> *Series* by Mary Pope Osborne. Jack and Annie, two normal kids from Frog Creek, Pennsylvania, are sent on adventures and missions with a magical tree house.

ADDITIONAL RESOURCES FOR INTERMEDIATE READERS

12 More Great Resources for Intermediate Readers, including Websites, Software, Games, Puzzles

These resources will help you further nurture and develop your child's reading skills and interests.

1. File Folders Game for reading by Marilyn Burch. These are fun little games. You will need File folders, glue, and tape. They are so worth the time it takes to put together though.

2. Franklin Kid Talking Dictionary and Spell Check Complete talking children's dictionary with 44,000 words, phonetic spell correction, interactive rhyme finder that speaks letters, words and definitions.

3. www.starfall.com is a free public service to teach children to read with phonics in conjunction with phonemic awareness practice. Perfect for preschool, kindergarten, first grade, second grade, special education, homeschool, and English language development.

4.	www.learninggamesforchildren.com
Online learning games and songs for kids that are fun, teach important skills for preschool and elementary school kids, and are free.

5.	The Reading Game Makes Learning To Read Fun, Fast and Effective with The Reading Game. These fast paced memory card games with accompanying content-rich storybooks can help any child learn to read without frustration.

6.	www.pbskids.org/beeswax/
Beeswax/PBS Kids Go! Focuses on current events. Its closed-captioning makes it a good tool for reading development.

7.	www.scholastic.com Fun activities for readers of all levels.

8.	www.thereadingplanet.com This site aims to motivate children to read.

9.	www.readingrocket.org Activities to help children learn to read.

10.	3-2-1 Contact A science magazine for the middle grades – following the PBS-TV format.

11. www.cricket.com Children's magazines.

12. Intothebook.com Exercises that help children learn reading.

PART FOUR

FOR ADVANCED READERS
3rd Through 6th Graders Reading Above Their Current Grade Level

CHARACTERISTICS OF ADVANCED READERS

Children who are reading above their grade level are considered advanced readers. These are children who learned to read easily, love books, and are voracious readers. They like discussing and sharing books they are reading or have read.

These children often spend hours reading for pleasure and are self-directed learners who have large vocabularies. They need little motivation to explore the world around them. The task for parents and teachers is to provide these children with books filled with ideas, a variety of literature, and challenging reading activities — that further nurture their reading achievement and curiosity about all things. Since these children are regarded as gifted readers, there are no milestones to assess year-end reading progress.

ACTIVITIES FOR ADVANCED READERS

12 Fun and Educational Games, Puzzles, and Other Activities for 3rd Graders – 6th Graders Reading Above Their Current Grade Level

These activities, games, and puzzles will challenge your advanced reader to develop higher levels of critical thinking and reasoning skills.

1. **Family Outing** – Have your child plan a family outing or a family vacation. Help her determine all the details she needs to cover when making this plan but then let her make the plan herself. Once she has the plan created, review it with her.

2. **Author Study** – Challenge your advanced reader by having him or her do an author study. Provide a selection of authors from which to choose. After selecting an author, your child or student needs to research the author, the history of his or her life and their culture, education, etc. The student would then write about how the author's life influenced their writing. Check your local library to see if any children's authors will

be making appearances there. If so, plan to attend these events with your child.

3.   **Character Time Travel** – Have your child or student select a character from a book she especially enjoyed. Tell her to take this character back in time to a different time period than the one in the book where the character lived. Have your child write about how this character would be different if he/she lived in this time period, and how the story would be different if it took place at this time.

4.   **New Endings** – Have your child create a new ending(s) to a popular story or book he really enjoyed reading.

5. **Mock Interview** – Have you child select a historical figure, such as a president, to interview. Tell your child he must use the Internet or books from the library to research information for a mock interview with this person. Have your child write down questions to ask the historical person,

then have the child write down the answers he thinks he would get if he really interviewed this person. After he has completed both the questions and the answers, have him read his "mock interview" to you and explain why he answered the questions the way he did.

6. **Plays** – Help your child write a short play to perform at home with siblings and friends or at school with classmates. Check out some Readers Theatre books from the library and first discuss what makes a good script for a play.

7. **Movie and Book Comparison** – Have your children or students choose a book that you will all read. After you've read the book, see the movie. Next, discuss the differences you found between the book and the movie. You can also have the children/students make a chart with these differences. The children might also tell which they preferred – the book or the movie – and give the reasons for their choices.

8. **Series Books** – Take your child to the bookstore or library and specifically look for

series books that might interest him/her. Have your child choose at least a couple of books in the series to read. Encourage him to get the next book in the series and read it each time he finishes another book in this series. From time to time, talk with your child about what he enjoys most about series books that isn't found in single title books.

9. **Time Period Research** – Have your child choose a specific time period in history that interests him. Help him research this time in history online by finding various websites related to this period. Have your child make notes about interesting information he finds out about this time period and discuss how he might use this information to create his own story.

10. **Hobbies** – Help your child discover a new hobby that involves reading as an integral part of this activity. Cooking (reading recipes), stamp collecting, travel, etc.

11. **Meal Planning and Preparation** – Have your child plan a meal and go online or use cookbooks to find recipes for each dish that be part of the meal. Then, supervise or help out as your child prepares this meal for your family.

12. **Movies** – Have your child look through the newspaper or online with you to choose a movie you can see together. Have him find out which theater to go to, what time the show is playing, and how much tickets cost. Have him explain why he chose this movie and why he thinks he made a wise choice. These kinds of critical skills and reasoning skills are important literacy skills as well.

SUGGESTED BOOKS FOR ADVANCED READERS

12 Popular or Classic Books for 3rd Graders – 6th Graders Who Are Reading Above Their Current Grade Level

It's always good to expose children to the classics. If your child attends public school, no doubt he will read some of the books on the following list as part of the regular curriculum. If you homeschool, be sure to include these classics in your own reading/language arts curriculum.

Other books on this list are not well-known classics, but they're wonderful stories children will enjoy and learn from.

1. The Pigman by Paul Zindel. Meet Mr. Pignati, a lonely old man with a beer belly and an awful secret. He's the Pigman, and he's got a great big twinkling smile. When John and Lorraine, two high school sophomores, meet Mr. Pignati, they learn his whole sad, zany story.

2. The Red Pony by John Steinbeck. Raised on a ranch in northern California, Jody is well-schooled in the hard work and

demands of a rancher's life. He is used to the way of horses, too; but nothing has prepared him for the special connection he will forge with Gabilan, the hot-tempered pony his father gives him.

3. Treasure Island by Robert Louis Stevenson. An exciting tale of pirates, buried treasure and danger.

4. A Day No Pigs Will Die by Robert Newton Peck. When twelve-year-old Robert saves a neighbor's cow from choking and helps it deliver a set of twin bull calves, he is given a small piglet as a reward. He grows to love this piglet and plans to keep it for a very long time and make a brood sow out of her. But things happen and he can't follow through with these plans and he has to learn some tough lessons about real life.

5. A Wrinkle in Time by Madeleine L'Engle. The Mury children fight to free their father from an evil presence.

6. The Secret Garden by Frances Hodgson Burnett. Mary Lennox loses her parents in an earthquake and is sent to England to live with her reclusive uncle. She discovers

a bedridden cousin and a secret garden.

7. Tuck Everlasting by Natalie Babbit. The story of a girl named Winnie who meets the Tucks, a family with a secret.

8. The Wind in The Willows by Kenneth Grahame. A collection of adventures that combine to tell the story of a group of everyday English animals who live along the banks of the River.

9. Strawberry Girl by Lois Lenski. Birdie Boyer was a Florida Cracker. She belonged to a large family who raised strawberries for a living. Birdie dreamed of getting an education and learning to play the organ.

10. Airball: My Life in Briefs by L.D. Harkrader. A modern day version of The Emperor's New Clothes.

11. The Giver by Lois Lowry. When Jonas turns twelve he is singled out to receive special training from The Giver.

12. A Northern Light by Jennifer Donnelly. Sixteen-year-old Mattie Gokey takes a job at the Glenmore Hotel. One of the guests

asks her to burn a secret bundle of letters. But when the guest drowns in the lake, Mattie discovers that the letters could reveal the grim truth behind a murder.

ADDITIONAL RESOURCES FOR ADVANCED READERS

12 More Great Resources for Advanced Readers, including Websites, Software, Games, Puzzles

Advanced readers need to be more sophisticated reading materials and resources to fulfill their needs to be challenged when learning.

1. <u>Nature Connection</u> The Nature Connection: An Outdoor Workbook for Kids, Families and Classrooms by Clare Walker Leslie. An interactive workbook chockfull of creative exercises for kids ages 8 to 13.

2. <u>The Geek Dad's Guide to Weekend Fun</u> by Ken Denmead. Filled with projects on how to make homemade robots from scratch, write and direct simple stop-motion movies and hack into mechanical toys to add cool electronic twists, and more.

3. Boggle, Scrabble, Thread Words -These board games are perfect for the entire family and will help children develop literacy skills. Available at Wal-Mart, Target, and other discount stores, as well

as online at amazon.com.

4. To help encourage your child to cultivate a hobby, subscribe to one or two hobby related or special interest magazines that are appropriate for children. Such as:

    a. Model Trains www.**modelrailroad**er.com
    b. Coin Collecting www.numismaster.com
    c. Stamp Collecting secretsto**stampcollecting**.com/mem bers
    d. Airplanes www.modelplanes.com
    e. Dog's World dog-world-magazine.com
    f. Cat Fancy www.catfancy.com

5. Visit these time period websites with your child for information needed to complete some of the activities suggested (in the previous sections of this book) for advanced readers:

    a. Ellis Island www.ellisisland.org
    b. National World War I Museum www.theworldwar.org
    c. Imperial War Museum

www.iwm.org.uk
- d. Gettysburg National Military Park
www.nps.gov/gett
- e. Little bighorn Battlefield National
Monument www.nps.gov/libi

6. National Geographic for Kids.
www.nationalgeograhic.com/kids
Games, Animals, Photos, Stories, and
More.

7. The British Museum of Ancient
Civilizations.
www.ancientcivilizations.co.uk. Where
Kids Can Learn about Ancient
Civilizations.

8. California Learning Strategies Center,
www.learningstrategiescenter.com. Advice
for Parents of Advanced Writers/Readers,
Math & Science

9. Find Age-Appropriate Books for Advanced
Readers.
www.scholastic.com/resources/article/bo
oks-for-kids. Some books for children can
be inappropriate. Find out what to do
when your advanced reader makes a ques-
tionable choice.

10. Reading Strategies for Advanced Primary
Readers. Request a copy from
www.gted@tea.state.tx.us. This publication

expands the knowledge about the characteristics and needs of advanced and gifted readers.

11. Smithsonian Kids
www.smithsonianeducation.org/students/
Educational Site for Kids from Smithsonian Magazine

12. American Museum of Natural History
www.amnh.org
Institution for scientific research and education, with a collection of more than 32 million specimens and artifacts. Includes a visitor's guide and collection details.

PART FIVE

FOR STRUGGLING READERS

Kindergarten Through 6th Graders Reading Below Their Current Grade Level

Children who are considered struggling readers have difficulty reading grade level fiction and non-fiction materials.

CHARACTERISTICS OF STRUGGLING READERS

Children who are struggling to read have missed, or failed to learn, important skills. To successfully bring children, who are not yet reading at their respective grade levels, a review of important reading skills needs to take place.

In particular, a review of letter names and sounds. Parents and teacher need to know whether their struggling readers knows all the letter names and sounds of the twenty six letters of the alphabet

A good way to assess letter name/sound knowledge is with flash cards. These can be purchased at a local bookstore, teacher supply store, or online.

Review Sight Words. 'Sight Words' are those words that should be recognized instantly. Examples of sight words are: this, are, to, of, in, etc. These words are often referred to as the most often used words found in sentences, or words most repeated throughout sentences. Skilled readers instantly recognize these words without hesitation.

Again, packages of sight words can be purchased at a local bookstore, teacher supply store, or online.

Repeat the same process that's used to assess letter name/sound knowledge. Once again those sight word not automatically recognized immediately need to be re-taught until they are memorized.

A review of blending sounds into words. Every good reader is capable of sounding out an unknown word. This is referred to as a 'word attack' skill. Good readers possess this reading ability. That is, they are capable of sounding out each letter within a word, in order to pronounce the entire word. This reading skill is absolutely necessary. Why? Because when children sound out words which are also in their listening vocabulary, they then understand what they are reading—and learn.

There are numerous written materials and software products available to teach children how to sound out. Parents and teachers can re-teach this reading skill. A variety of reading practice books and software products are available. Again, check local bookstores, teacher stores and online sources.

Paired Reading – Fun Reading Activity for Struggling Readers to Increase Sight Word and Reading Comprehension

Struggling readers need a thorough one-on-one review of phonics lessons, additional instruction on developing better comprehension, in both fiction and non-fiction materials, and drills to develop automaticity. That is, the ability to instantly recognize the most common words used in sentences, such as, can, it, the, was, are, etc.

Although, re-teaching and reviewing important reading skills are all necessary components to helping struggling readers improve their reading, supplementary reading activities should also be fun and motivating.

Paired Reading, is an activity parents, teachers and even a classmate can do with a child who is struggling to learn to read. One-on-one time, with a more capable reader, is not only effective but is an activity that is enjoyable and encouraging for struggling readers.

Here's how paired reading works. It's simple. A more capable reader reads aloud while the less capable reader, the struggling reader, follows along.

Here are six steps to follow when pair reading:

1. Select a book or story at your child's instructional level. This means a book or story your child can read, but has not mastered.

2. Preview the book or story with your child. Look at any visual clues such as illustrations or chapter headings.

3. Set a purpose for reading. Encourage struggling readers to make predictions about what is going to be read. A good prompt is, "after seeing the pictures what do you think this stories going to be about"? Or, after previewing this chapter what do think we're going to read about.

4. Finger Point. Make sure the struggling reader follows along with his or her finger, pointing under each word as it's being read aloud. Seeing words while simultaneously hearing them helps children develop sight word vocabulary.

5. Accurate Reading. Read aloud with accuracy and expression in your voice. Remember to read slowly enough so the struggling reader can see and hear each word simultaneously.

6. Textbook Paired Reading. When parents and teachers read textbook passages with their struggling readers. Begin by reading the assessment questions found at the end the chapter. As you pair read stop periodically. Discuss and decide whether what has been read so far, has answered any of the end-of-the-chapter questions. Repeat this process until the end of the text.

Variations of paired reading are when: Both the parent, teacher, or a fellow classmate and the struggling reader, read an identical passage aloud, together. Or, when the parent, teacher, or classmate turns with the struggling at reading aloud. Paired reading is also a good reading activity to help struggling readers develop better reading comprehension. Why? Because the better reader is doing the work of reading the words.

This allows the struggling reader to focus on the meaning within the printed words. As a rule, stories are most often used in pair reading sessions. However, textbook chapters and other information passages can be pair read, as well.

There are thousands of activities developed to help children learn to read. Paired Reading is an activity parents, teachers, and even classmates can perform to help struggling readers become better and confident readers, while exposing the enjoyment of reading.

"If done in a supportive, non-threatening way, students' read-aloud activities can enhance their interest and enjoyment of reading, improve fluency, increase vocabulary, and add to their storehouse of knowledge and concepts." (Teaching Reading in The 21st Century, 2007)

Read As Fast As You Can – Repeated Readings Increases Sight Word Recognition

Every good reader must read quickly with accuracy. Struggling readers need to improve both. An activity that is effective at achieving both, while motivating is called 'Repeated Readings'.

What you'll need:

- A Stop Watch
- A written passage that your child or student can read easily
- Graph Paper

The activity goes like this:

1. Have your child read these passage as fast as they can out loud. Record how many mistakes he or she makes the first time.

2. Log the time (minutes or seconds) it took to read the passage.

3. Point out all words missed and graph this data.

4. Child reads the passage again.
5. Repeat this process three to five times, always graphing the times and missed words.

Struggling readers immediately see their reading is improving. The graphed data shows their progress. Competition is always fun, so doing repeated readings encourages your child or student to set a goal, such as: "I'm going to read the passage in forty-five seconds with only two reading mistakes."

'Read Fast As You Can', repeated readings, helps children increase their instant sight word recognition, improve their ability to read words accurately, and boosts their self-esteem about their reading ability.

ACTIVITIES FOR STRUGGLING READERS

12 Fun and Educational Games, Puzzles, and Other Activities for Kindergarten Through 6th Graders Reading Below Their Current Grade Level

Struggling readers may be very resistant to sitting down with a book, so try some of these other activities that will help him improve his reading skills.

1. **Flashcards** – Have flash card practice become a regular part of homework time. To make it fun, set a timer and see how many words or letters on flash cards your child can recognize within a set period of time.

2. **Reading Scavenger Hunt** – Make a game by having your child discover all kinds of things in our daily life that require reading – have him make a list of all these items. If you have more than one child, have each child make a list and then compare their lists when they have compiled them.

3. **Everyday Reading** – Encourage your child to read anything and everything – from the backs of cereal boxes and labels on canned goods to traffic signs, billboards, menus at restaurants, etc. Constant practice will help your child become a better reader. And helping him see the need for reading in daily life will make him understand how reading can enrich his life.

If you make reading part of his everyday routine, soon his reading skills will improve.

4. **Daily newspaper** – subscribe to your local newspaper. Every morning before or after breakfast (or after school if you don't have time for this in the mornings), have your child choose one article of interest in the paper that he would like you to read to him or he would like to read aloud to you. Then discuss what was read.

5. **Shared Reading** – Read a book together. Get two copies of the same book. You read a page aloud, then let your child read the next page aloud. Alternately read like this for short periods

of time each day, until you've read the entire book together. Then talk about what you read.

6. **Field Trip** – Take a trip to your local museum or an art gallery together. Encourage your child to read the signs for the exhibits as sort of a treasure hunt for interesting information. If you are familiar with this exhibit, make a list of questions ahead of time that your child can look for answers to once he gets to the museum.

Note: Look online for information about the exhibit. You might find enough information there to generate some questions.

7. **Dinner Dates** – Go out to dinner (or breakfast or lunch) together – just you and your child. Have your child suggest something for you to order from the menu. Have him read the description of the item on the menu to you and tell why he thinks you would like this item.

8. **Grocery Shopping** – Make a grocery list for the week with your child. Look in the refrigerator,

pantry, and kitchen cabinets and call out the names of the items you need to buy and have your child write them down (help with the spelling if your child has trouble with some of the words). Next, go to the store with your child and let him find the items in the store.

9. **Vocabulary Notebook** – Have your child keep a vocabulary notebook of interesting new words he encounters during the day. If he doesn't know the meaning of a particular word – or how to pronounce it – when he sees it in print, help him look it up in the dictionary and learn to pronounce it and define it.

10. **Cooking or Baking** – Give your child the recipe for his favorite cookies, cake, or other food. Help him prepare this item himself by following the recipe.

11. **Word Practice** – Have your child practice writing words on a dry erase board at regular practice sessions during the week while you call

out the words to him or show them to him on flash cards.

13.   **Textbook Scavenger Hunt**   – Have a scavenger hunt using a textbook. But don't develop your questions from the general text. Instead, generate questions from pictures, captions, charts and graphs, headlines, subheads, sidebars, etc. Have your child look through these items in the text to get the answers to a list of questions you have created.

SUGGESTED BOOKS FOR STRUGGLING READERS

12 Popular or Classic Books for 3rd Graders – 6th Graders Who Are Reading Below Their Current Grade Level

Struggling readers may not be reading at their current grade level, but they are still interested in the same topics as children who are reading at or above grade level. For that reason, it's important to help your child choose books that are written at his current reading level yet appeal to his current interest level.

Provide this group of students with a selection of books that interest them, such as: humorous books, comic books, joke books, magazines, cartoons, nature and animals. Girls who are struggling to read are interested in teen magazines, pop culture, clothing, and jewelry.
Here are some books that have a lower reading level but higher interest level.

1. The Barn by Avi. (3rd grade reading level, 5th grade interest level) The schoolmaster says nine-year-old Benjamin is the finest student he's ever seen-fit for more than farming; destined for

great things. But his father's grave illness brings Ben home from school.

2. <u>Superfudge</u> by Judy Blume. (2nd grade reading level; 2–4th interest level) Peter is a sixth grade student who lives in New York City. He has a little brother, fondly known as Fudge. Peter's mom is going to be having another baby. Peter worries the new baby will create the same problems for him as fudge, and he plans to run away.

3. <u>Tales of a Fourth Grade Nothing</u> by Judy Blume. (3rd grade reading level; 3–5th interest level) Peter Hatcher feels like a fourth grade nothing.

4. <u>Socks</u> by Beverly Cleary.
    (2nd grade reading level; 3–5th interest level). A story of life with a baby from a cat's point of view.

5. <u>The Whipping Boy</u> by Sid Fleischman.
    (3rd grade reading level; 3–5th grade interest level) A bratty prince and his whipping boy have many adventures when they inadvertently trade places after becoming involved with dangerous outlaws.

6. The Trouble With Perfect by Mary E. Ryan. (3rd grade reading level; 6–12 interest level). Thirteen-year-old Kyle, who is hopeless in math, is tempted to cheat on an exam to please his demanding, heavily drinking father.

7. The Time Warp Series by Jon Scieszka. (3rd grade reading level; 3rd – 6th grade interest level) Three friends are transported through time by a magic book.

8. Dog Years by Sally Warner.(3rd grade reading level; 4–6 grade interest level)A humorous story and cartoon drawings chronicle the joys, hardships, and tribulations of middle-school life.

9. Because of Winn Dixie by Kate DiCamillo. Ten-year-old India Opal Buloni lives in the town of Naomi, Florida. All sorts of good things happen to her when she adopts an ugly dog she finds in the Winn-Dixie grocery story.

10. Fair Weather In 1893, thirteen-year-old Rosie and members of her family travel from their Illinois farm to Chicago to visit Aunt Euterpe. They go to the World's

Columbian Exposition, where they encounter Buffalo Bill and Lillian Russell.

11. Snow Treasure by Marie McSwigan. An actual incident in which Norwegian children smuggled gold past the Nazis is the basis for this story.

12. Deltora Quest by Emily Rodda. The adventures of Lief, Barda, and Jasmine as they search for the seven magic jewels of the Belt of Deltora in order to save their country and its people from the evil Shadow Lord

Texting

Today, nearly every school-age child is familiar with cellphone texting. High tech electronic gadgets are part of children's lives. Although, texting has received negative press, this new convenience is helping children learn to read, and show the importance of being able to read. Parents and teachers need to take advantage of this new form of media, and turn it into a reading lesson.

Try This: Have your struggling reader text you a message. Text the same message back, although add onto the initial text sentence. Text back and forth adding new words your child needs to be able to read. Also, periodically introduce new words into your texts, to expand your child's or student's vocabulary.

ADDITIONAL RESOURCES FOR STRUGGLING READERS

12 More Great Resources for Struggling Readers, including Websites, Software, Games, Puzzles, etc.

Struggling readers need regular opportunities for reading and practicing skills that will help them become better readers. Try these resources:

1. www.rainbowreading.com Rainbow Reading Games and Phonics Games. Games on basic initial letter practice, word building, common letter patterns, and more than 30 board games that practice more advanced letter patterns and skills. Also includes games that teach and review antonyms, synonyms, prefixes, suffixes, compound words, contractions, plurals and homophones.

2. www.readingblueprint.com Reading Blueprint Software. Before you consider paying for the programs designed to help your struggling reader(s), sign up for the free book and bonus guides in the right sidebar of the homepage of this site.

3. www.readingrockets.com Reading Rockets has helpful articles about why some children struggle with reading:

4. www.pcieducation.com PCI Education provides materials for struggling readers and struggling learners.

5. http://www.merrybee.info/lang/langcom.html. Merry Lee Presents provides free printable worksheets and online comprehension exercises. Other literacy topics include reading strategies, phonics, grammar, and websites for teachers.

6. http://unlocktheeinsteininside.com/ Learning RX - braining training procedure and free downloads to help children become better learners and readers.

7. http://www.readingupgrade.com/html/ruhome.htm. Reading Upgrade provides online lessons filled with songs, video, and games to teach basic reading for student grades 3 to 12 and adults reading below Grade 5 level.

8. www.athome.readinghorizons.com Best online reading games - from The Reading

Corner provides online reading games with plenty of fun online games to help your child improve his reading skills.

9. www.learningally.org Learning Ally.org Accessible materials for individuals with visual and learning disabilities.

10. http://www.betterchildrensbooks.com/onlinereading-games.html/ Fun Online Reading Games for Kids

11. http://www.mcauliffe.brevard.k12.fl.us Online Educational Games/ Activities and more.

12. http://www.k5stars.com/salescbank/sales2.php?hop=sandykc K-5 Stars Online Educational games for kids

ABOUT THE AUTHOR

Carol Fraser Hagen is a former public school K-12 Reading Specialist and now tutors children and adults with language learning difficulties. She holds a Master's degree in Special Reading and an Educational Specialist degree in Curriculum and Instruction and is a certified instructor in the Orton-Gillingham Multi-Sensory Reading Method.

Hagen was the recipient of the Shawnee Mission Education Foundation's Grant for developing "Talking Books", a finalist in the 2008 Society of Children's Book Writers and Illustrators "Work in Progress Grant", for her research work, and she is a published children's writer.

Hagen's articles and curricular materials have been published in the Missouri Chapter of the International Reading Association—The Missouri Reader, Kansas City Parent, Apex Learning, A Pass Education and other print and online publications. She writes curriculum, articles on how to teach and learn how to read, and instructional strategies to help parents and teachers of dyslexic children.

Her website is www.carolfraserhagen.com
Sign up for her weekly newsletter and receive a FREE e-book, *Ten Reasons to Read Aloud.*

BIBLIOGRAPHY

Adams, Marilyn, Jager "What about Knowledge of Nursery Rhymes?" *Beginning To Read: Thinking and Learning about Print.* University of Illinois Urbana-Champaign: Center for the Study of Reading The Reading Research and Education Center, 1990. 42-45. Print.

Anderson, Hiebert, Scott, et. al.. *A Nation of Readers: The Report of the Commission of Reading.* National Institute of Education, U.S. Department of Education. Washington D.C., 1985.

Clark, Virginia P., Paul A. Eschholz, and Alfred F. Rosa. *Language: Introductory Readings.* New York: St. Martin's, 19994. Print.

Farstrup, Alan E., and S. Jay. Samuels. *What Research Has to Say about Reading Instruction.* Newark, DE: International Reading Association, 2002. Print.

Faver, Sherri. "Repeated Reading of Poetry Can Enhance Reading Fluency." *The Reading Teacher* 62.4 (2008): 350-52. Print.

Grandin, Temple. "My Experience with Visual Thinking Sensory Problems and Communication Difficulties." MAAPing the Future Conference. Hilton, Indianapolis. 15 Sept. 1995. Speech.

Henry, Marcia K. "The Decoding/spelling Curriculum: Integrated Decoding and Spelling Instruction from Pre-school to Early Secondary School." *Dyslexia* 3.3 (1997): 178-89. Print.

Heward, William L., and Michael D. Orlansky. *Exceptional Children: An Introductory Survey of Special Education.* New York: Merrill, 1992. Print.

Hickman, Peggy, and Sharolyn D. Pollard-Durodola. *Dynamic Read-aloud Strategies for English Learners: Building Language and Literacy in the Primary Grades.* Newark, DE: International Reading Association, 2009. Print.

Mesmer, Heidi Anne E., and Priscilla L. Griffith. "Everybody's Selling It—But Just What Is Explicit, Systematic Phonics Instruction?" *The Reading Teacher* 59.4 (2005): 366-76. Print.

Minskoff, Esther H. *Teaching Reading to Struggling Readers*. Baltimore, Mayland: Paul H. Brooks, 2005. Print.

Pressley, Michael, Kristen Bogner, Lisa M. Raohael, and Sara Dolezal. "Balance Literacy Instruction." *Special Education Policy and Practice: Accountability, Instruction, and Social Challenges*. Ed. Alysia Roehrig. Denver, CO: Love, 2004. 267-85. Print.

Pikulski, John J., and David J. Chard. "Fluency: Bridge Between Decoding and Reading Comprehension." *The Reading Teacher* 58.6 (2005): 510-19. Print.

Pinnel, Gay Su. "Children's Early Literacy" Learning: Literacy Research Paper. Scholastic Inc. 1994. Print.

Radencich, Marguerite C., and Jeanne Shay Schumm. "Above Average Readers." *A Handbook For the K-12 Reading Resource Specialist*. Ed. Penny C. Beers. Boston, MA: Allyn and Bacon, 1993. 93-97. Print.

Skrtic, Thomas M., Karen R. Harris, and James G. Shriner. *Special Education Policy and*

Practice: Accountability, Instruction, and Social Challenges. Denver, CO: Love Pub., 2005. Print

Strickland, Dorothy, S. and Morrow, Lesley, Mandel. *Emerging Literacy: Young Children Learn to Read and Write*

Strickland, Dorothy S. "Learning Phonics: Strategies That Support Beginning Readers and Writers." *Teaching Phonics Today: A Primer for Educators.* Newark, DE: International Reading Association, 1998. 53-65. Print.

Waring, Cynthia Conway. *Developing Independent Readers: Strategy-oriented Reading Activities for Learners with Special Needs.* West Nyack, NY: Center for Applied Research in Education, 1995. Print.

Printed in Great Britain
by Amazon